Hemp in The Houses

Hemp in The Houses

AN ASTROLOGICAL ADVENTURE
THROUGH THE CANNABIS GALAXY

Matthew Petchinsky

Apophis Enterprises LLC

≈

Hemp in The Houses: An Astrological Adventure Through the Cannabis Galaxy
By: Matthew Petchinsky

Introduction 1A

Astrology has been a fascination for thousands of years, there are many different versions of it and it has had the hearts and mind of man in every culture on Earth, since mankind was primitive Caveman in a cave to Egyptian to modern man. Astrology is engrained in our DNA. Please enjoy this book.

Introduction: The Cosmic Canvas of Cannabis

In the boundless expanse of the cosmos, where stars whisper secrets to the void, and planets dance in the harmony of unseen forces, there exists a galaxy not mapped by ordinary stargazers. It is a place where the celestial and the terrestrial merge, where the mystic energies of the cosmos infuse themselves into the very essence of existence. This is the Cannabis Galaxy, a realm where the ancient and venerable plant of hemp resides not just as a physical entity, but as a cosmic symbol, intertwined with the very fabric of astrology.

Our journey begins on the Cosmic Canvas of Cannabis, an enchanting prelude that sets the stage for an adventure across this celestial landscape. Here, hemp is not merely a plant but a protagonist in a saga that spans the ages, its destiny entwined with the stars themselves. This voyage invites you to explore the mystical origins of hemp, perceived since ancient times as a conduit to the divine, a plant with the power to unlock the secrets of the universe and establish a profound connection with the celestial realms.

Ancient civilizations looked to the heavens for guidance, seeing the patterns of stars as omens and messages from the gods. Among these celestial signs, they recognized hemp as a gift from the cosmos, a plant bestowed with sacred properties, capable of healing, enlightening, and connecting the human spirit to the greater universe. Astrologers of old charted the skies, finding in the movements of planets and stars, alignments that echoed the cycles of planting, harvesting, and utilizing hemp, imbuing these activities with spiritual significance.

The story of hemp is as old as the stars themselves. Mythologies from various cultures have hinted at its cosmic origin, suggesting that this plant was sown on Earth by star beings or created from the very dust of shooting stars, making its fibers resonate with stellar energies. These ancient beliefs laid the groundwork for an astrological adventure, one that sees hemp as a celestial navigator, guiding humanity through the ebbs and flows of existence with the wisdom of the universe woven into its very DNA.

As we embark on this journey through the Cannabis Galaxy, we delve into the heart of astrology, where each sign, each planet, and each house in the zodiac becomes a chapter in the epic story of hemp. From the fiery ambition of Aries to the watery depths of Pisces, hemp's influence spreads, shaping destinies and aligning with the cosmic forces that govern life itself. This adventure is not just about understanding hemp's place in the world but rediscovering our connection to the cosmos, a reminder that we, like hemp, are made of stardust, destined to navigate the mysteries of the universe together.

So, let us begin this astrological adventure, stepping onto the Cosmic Canvas of Cannabis with open minds and hearts, ready to explore the galaxy where the ancient and the celestial intertwine. Through the lens of astrology, we will discover the unique role hemp plays in the cosmic scheme, unraveling the celestial connections that have guided its journey through time and space. This is not just a story of a plant but a cosmic voyage that invites us to see the universe in a new light, through the green leaves of hemp, the star-child of the Cannabis Galaxy.

If you want to see some amazing products, please visit my Virtual Dispensary: https://shift.store/sg1fan23477/retail

Chapter 1: Hemp and the Harmonics of the Universe

In the grand tapestry of the cosmos, where each thread is infused with the essence of the stars, hemp has been woven into the fabric of human history as a symbol of unity between the Earth and the heavens. This chapter delves into the ancient belief systems and cultures that revered hemp as not just a plant of earthly origin but as a sacred emblem, intertwined with celestial wisdom and cosmic energy. It explores the universal significance of hemp, highlighting its role in rituals and medicine across civilizations, and how it served as a bridge between the terrestrial and the astral.

The Sacred Strands of History

The story of hemp's sacred connection to the cosmos unfurls across the tapestry of ancient civilizations. From the steppes of Central Asia, where it was first cultivated nearly 10,000 years ago, to the banks of the Nile, the gardens of Babylon, and the sacred sites of the Americas, hemp has been revered as a gift from the celestial realms. The ancient Chinese, for instance, believed that the hemp plant was imbued with yin and yang, its fibers representing the fundamental duality and balance of the universe. It was used in rituals to honor the heavens, in the weaving of burial shrouds to connect the deceased with the cosmic cycle, and in medicine as a conduit of healing energies from the stars.

Similarly, in the Vedic texts of ancient India, cannabis (a close relative of hemp) was celebrated as one of the five sacred plants. It was believed that a guardian angel resided in its leaves, linking the plant to the divine. The consumption of cannabis in religious ceremonies was thought to cleanse the soul and bring the devotee closer to the gods, illustrating the plant's role as a spiritual bridge between the cosmos and the earthly realm.

Celestial Rhythms in the Planting and Harvesting

The cultivation of hemp itself was guided by the stars. Farmers across ancient civilizations would plant and harvest according to the celestial calendar, aligning their agricultural practices with the rhythms of the universe. The planting of hemp seeds with the new moon and the harvesting under the full moon were common practices, rooted in the belief that the phases of the moon affected the growth and potency of the plant. This harmonious relationship between the cycles of hemp and the celestial bodies underscored the plant's connection to the cosmic dance of the universe.

Hemp in Rituals and Medicine: A Universal Bridge

Hemp's role in rituals and medicine across cultures further highlights its significance as a universal symbol of the connection between the earth and the stars. In ancient Egypt, hemp was used in the production of papyrus and also served as a key ingredient in medicinal remedies for a variety of ailments, symbolizing the transfer of celestial healing powers to the earthly domain. In Europe, during the Middle Ages, hemp was used in ceremonies to protect against evil spirits, its smoke believed to carry prayers and intentions to the celestial realms.

The Native American tribes also held hemp in high regard, using it in sacred ceremonies to communicate with the spirit world. They believed that the plant had the power to open doorways to higher realms of consciousness, facilitating a deeper understanding of the mysteries of the universe.

The Cosmic Symphony

As we explore the ancient belief systems and the multifaceted roles of hemp in rituals and medicine, it becomes evident that hemp served as a key instrument in the cosmic symphony, harmonizing the energies of the earth and the stars. Its presence in diverse cultures and civilizations as a sacred plant, a healer, a protector, and a guide, underscores its universal significance. Hemp, with its celestial origins and earthly manifestations, represents the harmonics of the universe, a resonant link between the microcosm and the macrocosm, the individual and the infinite.

In this journey through the harmonics of the universe, hemp emerges not merely as a plant of practical utility but as a symbol of cosmic connection, a reminder of the intricate dance between the material and the mystical, the earthly and the ethereal. As we continue our astrological adventure through the Cannabis Galaxy, we carry with us the knowledge of hemp's ancient legacy, its role in the harmonics of the universe, and its power to bridge the divide between the earth and the stars, guiding us toward a deeper understanding of our place in the cosmos.

If you want to see some amazing products, please visit my Virtual Dispensary: https://shift.store/sg1fan23477/retail

Chapter 2: Aries - The Trailblazer's Torch

In the cosmic journey through the Cannabis Galaxy, we next arrive at the constellation of Aries, the first sign of the zodiac, symbolizing new beginnings and raw, untamed energy. Aries, ruled by Mars, the planet of war and energy, embodies the spirit of the warrior, the pioneer, always ready to blaze new trails and conquer uncharted territories. This chapter explores how Aries, the initiator, utilizes the fiery energy of hemp strains to fuel their ventures, overcome challenges, and ignite their pioneering spirit.

The Fiery Symbiosis

Aries individuals are known for their dynamic energy, courage, and determination. They are trailblazers at heart, often the first to venture into the unknown. The fiery energy of certain hemp strains resonates with the innate qualities of Aries, providing the perfect catalyst to ignite their adventurous spirit and bolster their natural courage. These strains are not just tools but allies in Aries' relentless quest for new horizons.

Hemp Strains that Stoke the Aries Flame

To complement the bold nature of Aries, hemp strains with uplifting and energizing effects are recommended. Strains like Sour Diesel, known for its invigorating cerebral high, and Green Crack, with its sharp energy and focus, are particularly suited to the Aries temperament. These strains can enhance Aries' natural zest for life, fueling their endless appetite for adventure and helping them to overcome obstacles with renewed vigor.

Adventure Awaits: Activities for Aries

For Aries, adventure is not just an activity but a way of life. Harnessing the power of hemp, they can embark on journeys that not only challenge their physical limits but also expand their horizons. Activities such as hiking to the peak of a towering mountain, engaging in extreme sports, or exploring the wilderness are where Aries truly shines. These adventures, enhanced by the energizing effects of hemp, allow Aries to experience the thrill of the conquest and the joy of discovery.

Cultivating Courage: Hemp as a Catalyst

In the face of challenges, Aries can rely on the empowering properties of hemp to fortify their resolve. Whether it's embarking on a solo journey across foreign lands, starting a new venture, or standing up for their beliefs, Aries can draw on the strength of hemp to maintain their courage and determination. By aligning their endeavors with the energetic vibrations of specific hemp strains, Aries can transform obstacles into stepping stones on their path to success.

Meditative Fires: Igniting Inner Wisdom

Despite their outward focus on action and conquest, Aries can also benefit from the introspective qualities of hemp. Engaging in meditative practices, fueled by strains that promote clarity and insight, can help Aries connect with their inner wisdom. This introspection is crucial for Aries, allowing them to channel their boundless energy with intention and purpose, ensuring that their fiery spirit leads them not just to adventure, but to meaningful discoveries about themselves and the world around them.

Conclusion: The Trailblazer's Journey

As Aries harnesses the fiery energy of hemp, they illuminate the path not only for themselves but for others to follow. Their pioneering spirit, fueled by the potent synergy between their natural qualities and the empowering effects of hemp, enables them to overcome challenges and blaze new trails. In the Cannabis Galaxy, Aries stands as a testament to the power of initiative, courage, and the relentless pursuit of adventure. With hemp as their torch, Aries continues to lead the way, exploring new frontiers and inspiring all who cross their path to embrace the journey of discovery.

If you want to see some amazing products, please visit my Virtual Dispensary: https://shift.store/sg1fan23477/retail

Chapter 3: Taurus - The Sensualist's Sanctuary

As our celestial voyage through the Cannabis Galaxy unfolds, we find ourselves under the starlit sky of Taurus, the zodiac's sensualist and guardian of earthly delights. Governed by Venus, the planet of love, beauty, and pleasure, Taurus is the embodiment of desire for comfort, stability, and the pleasures of the senses. This chapter explores Taurus's deep-rooted connection to the earth, mirrored in the grounding properties of hemp, and offers suggestions for indulgent, sensory-enhancing hemp strains and relaxation rituals that cater to Taurus's love for comfort and luxury.

Grounding in the Garden of the Earth

Taurus thrives in the lushness of nature's bounty, finding solace and joy in the textures, flavors, and aromas that the earth offers. This tactile connection to the world is a source of deep pleasure and grounding for Taurus, reflecting their intrinsic desire for stability and serenity. Hemp, with its earthy roots and multifaceted benefits, serves as a natural ally for Taurus, enhancing their connection to the earth and providing a foundation for relaxation and indulgence.

Hemp Strains for the Taurus Palette

To satisfy Taurus's penchant for the finer things, certain hemp strains stand out for their ability to enhance sensory experiences and promote relaxation. Strains like Granddaddy Purple, with its sweet, berry-like aroma, and Bubba Kush, known for its rich, chocolatey undertones, are perfect for Taurus. These strains not only delight the senses but also offer a deep, grounding relaxation that envelops Taurus in the comfort they cherish.

Luxurious Relaxation Rituals

For Taurus, relaxation is not just an activity but an art form, a ritualistic indulgence that engages all the senses. Incorporating hemp into these rituals can elevate their experience to new heights of luxury and comfort. A bath infused with hemp-derived bath bombs or oils, surrounded by the soft glow of candles and the soothing sounds of nature or gentle music, can provide the ultimate sanctuary for Taurus. Following this with a massage using hemp-based lotions or oils can further enhance their sensory journey, leaving them feeling pampered, relaxed, and deeply connected to their body and the earth.

The Culinary Delights of Hemp

Given Taurus's love for gastronomic pleasures, integrating hemp into culinary experiences can be a delightful exploration. Hemp seeds or oil can be incorporated into decadent recipes, offering a nutty, earthy flavor that complements Taurus's gourmet tastes. Whether it's a rich, chocolate hemp-infused dessert or a savory dish garnished with hemp seeds, these culinary creations can provide a unique sensory experience, combining the pleasures of taste with the grounding benefits of hemp.

Creating a Sanctuary of Serenity

For Taurus, creating a space that reflects their love for comfort, beauty, and the sensual pleasures of life is essential. Hemp can play a role in this, too, through the use of hemp-based fabrics and materials that offer both luxury and sustainability. A Taurus's living space, adorned with soft hemp linens, plush cushions, and warm, inviting textures, becomes a sanctuary of serenity, a retreat from the chaos of the world where they can recharge in the lap of luxury.

Conclusion: The Sensualist's Embrace of Hemp

In the realm of Taurus, hemp finds a special place as a companion in the pursuit of pleasure, relaxation, and sensory delight. Through indulgent strains, luxurious relaxation rituals, and the integration of hemp into culinary and domestic spheres, Taurus can deepen their connection to the earth and the pleasures it provides. In the Cannabis Galaxy, Taurus's journey with hemp is a celebration of the senses, an exploration of the depths of comfort and pleasure, and a testament to the grounding power of nature's bounty. As Taurus embraces the sensualist's sanctuary, they reaffirm their devotion to the beauty and richness of the earthly experience, guided by the stars and the steadfast companion that is hemp.

If you want to see some amazing products, please visit my Virtual Dispensary: https://shift.store/sg1fan23477/retail

Chapter 4: Gemini - The Conversationalist's Companion

Our celestial odyssey through the Cannabis Galaxy sails us into the realm of Gemini, the Twins, where the air is alive with the spark of intellect, wit, and the ceaseless exchange of ideas. Governed by Mercury, the messenger of the gods, Gemini embodies communication, duality, and the intellectual curiosity that drives the quest for knowledge and interaction. This chapter explores how Gemini's dual nature finds a kindred spirit in versatile hemp strains that stimulate conversation, creativity, and the social interplay that Geminis so dearly love. We will also delve into fun social games and intellectual explorations with hemp that enhance Gemini's communicative prowess and cater to their ever-curious mind.

Hemp Strains That Speak Gemini's Language

Gemini thrives on variety and mental stimulation, qualities that certain hemp strains can amplify, enhancing their natural proclivity for conversation and exploration. Strains such as Jack Herer, known for its cerebral elevation, and Super Lemon Haze, with its energizing and creative boost, are particularly suited to Gemini's lively spirit. These strains not only encourage a flow of ideas and conversation but also complement Gemini's versatility, offering a spectrum of experiences that can shift as swiftly as the winds of their thoughts.

Social Games and Cannabis: A Gemini Gathering

Geminis, the social butterflies of the zodiac, revel in gatherings that spark their intellectual curiosity and verbal dexterity. Incorporating hemp into social games can turn a simple get-together into a hive of animated discussion and laughter. Games like "Cannabis Charades," where participants act out different strains or cannabis-related activities, or "Puff, Puff, Pass the Story," where each puff inspires a new twist in a collectively told tale, can be both entertaining and stimulating for Gemini's quick mind.

The Intellectual Feast: Cannabis-Enhanced Explorations

Gemini's insatiable appetite for knowledge and discovery finds a perfect outlet in intellectual explorations enhanced by hemp. Organizing themed discussions or debates on topics ranging from the mysteries of the universe to the nuances of art, all while enjoying strains that sharpen the wit and open the mind, can be a delightful way for Geminis to engage and learn. Similarly, "Cannabis Book Clubs" where literary works are discussed under the gentle influence of strains that enhance perception and insight, can offer a new depth of appreciation and understanding.

Creative Workshops: Crafting and Cannabis

Gemini's love for creativity and their dexterous hands make them excellent craftsmen and artists. Hosting creative workshops, where participants can partake in arts and crafts while enjoying creativity-enhancing strains, provides a perfect playground for Gemini's multifaceted interests. Whether it's painting, writing poetry, or crafting DIY projects, these gatherings can spark inspiration, foster community, and provide a tangible outlet for Gemini's boundless energy and ideas.

Gemini's Digital Dialogues

In today's digital age, Gemini's communicative prowess can extend far beyond physical gatherings. Organizing virtual meet-ups or online game nights, where discussions or competitions take place over streams of conversation-boosting strains, can satisfy Gemini's craving for interaction and novelty. Platforms that allow for shared experiences, like watching movies together online or exploring virtual worlds, while engaging in stimulating conversation, can bridge distances and bring Geminis closer to their kindred spirits.

Conclusion: The Multiplicity of Gemini's Cannabis Experience

For Gemini, the Conversationalist's Companion, hemp offers a multifaceted mirror to their own nature, enhancing their ability to communicate, create, and connect. Through carefully selected strains that stimulate the mind and encourage dialogue, to social games and creative explorations that cater to their intellectual and artistic appetites, Gemini can find in cannabis a versatile ally. In the vast expanse of the Cannabis

Galaxy, Gemini's journey is a dance of interaction and curiosity, a voyage fueled by the synergistic energies of hemp and the mercurial spirit of the Twins. As Gemini continues to navigate the celestial currents of conversation and creativity, hemp remains their steadfast companion, enriching their adventures with the depth and diversity of the cosmos itself.

If you want to see some amazing products, please visit my Virtual Dispensary: https://shift.store/sg1fan23477/retail

5: Cancer - The Moonchild's Muse

As we drift further into the heart of the Cannabis Galaxy, we find ourselves enveloped in the comforting embrace of Cancer, the Moonchild. Ruled by the Moon, this sign embodies the essence of nurturing, protection, and deep emotional currents. Cancers are the caretakers of the zodiac, their hearts and homes a sanctuary for all. This chapter delves into how the nurturing and protective nature of Cancer finds solace in hemp strains that offer emotional and physical comfort. Additionally, we explore creative home-based cannabis rituals that enhance Cancer's intuitive connection with the moon and its phases, deepening their already profound bond with the celestial body that guides them.

Hemp Strains for the Moonchild's Heart

For Cancer, whose emotions ebb and flow like the tides, finding hemp strains that provide emotional balance and physical comfort is crucial. Strains such as Blue Dream, with its gentle euphoric lift and calming effects, or Northern Lights, known for its ability to relax the body and soothe the mind, resonate with Cancer's need for comfort and security. These strains act as a tender embrace, enveloping the Moonchild in a blanket of tranquility, offering solace from the outside world and aligning with their nurturing nature.

Lunar Rituals with Cannabis: Aligning with the Moon's Phases

Cancer's intuitive connection with the moon is a profound aspect of their being, influencing their moods, desires, and spiritual practices. Incorporating cannabis into lunar rituals can enhance this connection, turning routine practices into sacred ceremonies that honor the Moon's influence over their lives.

- **New Moon Rituals**: The New Moon marks a time for beginnings and intentions. Cancers can create a ritual around setting intentions for the lunar cycle ahead, perhaps writing these intentions down and then meditating on them while enjoying a calming strain. This practice can help manifest their desires, using the New Moon's energy to plant the seeds of future growth.

- **Full Moon Rituals**: The Full Moon is a time for release and reflection. Cancers can engage in a ritual of letting go, perhaps writing down what no longer serves them and burning the paper as a symbolic release, all while partaking in a strain that fosters introspection and emotional release. This ritual allows them to cleanse their emotional palette and make room for the new.

- **Cannabis-Infused Moon Water**: Charging water under the moonlight is a practice that aligns with Cancer's elemental nature. By infusing this moon water with hemp, either through direct infusion or by placing hemp seeds or leaves around the container, they can create a spiritually charged drink that nourishes their body and soul, harmonizing their energy with that of the moon.

- **Moon Gardens**: Cancers might consider cultivating a moon garden, planting herbs and flowers that bloom at night or that are traditionally associated with lunar energy, alongside their cannabis plants. This garden becomes a sacred space for nighttime reflection and relaxation, where the Moonchild can commune with the moon and the earth.

Creating a Sanctuary at Home

For Cancer, home is not just a place but a feeling. By incorporating cannabis into their home life, whether through aromatherapeutic cannabis-infused candles, hemp-based textiles that add comfort and warmth to their space, or simply by designating a special area for their lunar cannabis rituals, they create an environment that supports their emotional and spiritual well-being.

Conclusion: Cancer's Celestial Comfort

For Cancer, the Moonchild, cannabis is not just a plant but a muse, a companion that supports their emotional depth, nurtures their need for comfort, and enhances their connection to the celestial force that guides them. Through the thoughtful selection of strains that harmonize with their mood and the incorporation of cannabis into rituals that align with the moon's phases, Cancer can deepen their intuitive bond with the cosmos. In the Cannabis Galaxy, Cancer's journey is a voyage of emotional exploration, a quest for comfort and understanding in the arms of the moon, guided by the gentle influence of hemp.

If you want to see some amazing products, please visit my Virtual Dispensary: https://shift.store/sg1fan23477/retail

Chapter 6: Leo - The Sovereign's Spark

In the celestial dance through the Cannabis Galaxy, we next turn our gaze to the majestic constellation of Leo. Ruled by the Sun, the center of our solar system, Leo radiates warmth, vitality, and an undeniable charisma. This sign embodies the essence of leadership, creativity, and a generous spirit that seeks to inspire and uplift those around them. This chapter will explore how Leo's radiant energy and inherent leadership qualities are amplified by vibrant, uplifting hemp strains. Additionally, we will provide recommendations for hemp-infused social gatherings and self-expression activities that allow Leo's natural charisma and sovereign spirit to truly shine.

Hemp Strains that Ignite Leo's Fire

To match the vibrant energy of Leo, certain hemp strains stand out for their ability to uplift, energize, and inspire creativity. Strains like Super Silver Haze, with its euphoric and creative boost, and Tangie, known for its uplifting effects and citrus-flavored notes, resonate with Leo's sunny disposition. These strains can enhance Leo's natural enthusiasm, support their creative endeavors, and keep their spirits high, allowing them to lead and inspire with renewed vigor and passion.

The Regal Revelry: Hemp-Infused Gatherings

Leo thrives in the spotlight and enjoys being the life of the party, making them the perfect host for social gatherings that reflect their love for drama and flair. Hemp-infused dinner parties, where guests are treated to a menu of gourmet dishes incorporating hemp-based ingredients, can showcase Leo's generous nature and culinary creativity. To add to the festive atmosphere, a "Cannabis Cocktail Hour" featuring hemp-infused beverages can stir conversation and camaraderie among guests, setting the stage for an unforgettable evening where Leo's hospitality shines bright.

Creative Expression Under the Sun's Influence

Leo's creative energy, when channeled into self-expression, can produce works of art that captivate and inspire. Hemp strains that stimulate creativity can be the muse for Leo's artistic endeavors, whether it's painting, music, writing, or any form of artistic expression that allows them to convey their vibrant inner world. Hosting creative workshops or jam sessions where friends can come together to create and share their art can be a fulfilling way for Leo to express their creativity and encourage others to do the same.

Spotlight on Charisma: Performance and Presentation

Leo's natural charisma and love for performance find a perfect outlet in activities that place them center stage. Organizing open mic nights, stand-up comedy evenings, or theater productions infused with the creative and uplifting effects of hemp can provide Leo with the platform to dazzle and entertain. These events not only allow Leo to bask in the adoration they adore but also foster a sense of community and shared joy, reflecting Leo's underlying desire to uplift those around them.

Sunset Salutations: Yoga and Meditation

While Leo loves the limelight, they also benefit from moments of reflection to connect with their inner fire and maintain their regal poise. Engaging in sunset yoga sessions or meditation circles, especially when enhanced with strains known for their uplifting and introspective qualities, can provide Leo with the balance they need. These practices, set against the backdrop of the setting sun, can be a powerful ritual for Leo to recharge their solar energies and align with their sovereign essence.

Conclusion: Leo's Luminous Path

For Leo, the Sovereign's Spark, hemp serves as both a catalyst for creativity and a companion in their quest to inspire and lead. Through the careful selection of vibrant, uplifting strains and the integration of hemp into social gatherings, artistic expressions, and reflective practices, Leo can amplify their radiant energy and share their light with the world. In the Cannabis Galaxy, Leo's journey is marked by warmth, generosity, and the unyielding desire to shine brightly, illuminating the path for others to follow. With hemp as their ally, Leo's sovereign spirit remains undimmed, a beacon of inspiration and leadership under the cosmic sky.

If you want to see some amazing products, please visit my Virtual Dispensary: https://shift.store/sg1fan23477/retail

Chapter 7: Virgo - The Healer's Herb

As we continue our celestial journey through the Cannabis Galaxy, we arrive under the constellation of Virgo, the zodiac's emblem of meticulousness, health, and purity. Governed by Mercury, Virgo embodies the essence of analytical thought, practicality, and a profound connection to the physical body and its well-being. This chapter will delve into how Virgo's health-conscious and detail-oriented approach finds a harmonious alignment with hemp strains that promote wellness, purity, and balance. Furthermore, we will provide practical advice on integrating hemp into wellness routines, perfectly complementing Virgo's penchant for order, cleanliness, and self-improvement.

Hemp Strains for the Health-Conscious Virgo

For Virgo, the selection of hemp strains is a thoughtful process, emphasizing strains known for their cleanliness, purity, and medicinal properties. CBD-dominant strains like ACDC and Harlequin, renowned for their therapeutic effects without the psychoactive high, resonate with Virgo's preference for health over hedonism. These strains can offer relief from anxiety, inflammation, and pain, supporting Virgo's meticulous care of their physical and mental well-being.

Integrating Hemp into Virgo's Wellness Routine

Virgo's wellness routine is a testament to their belief in the virtue of self-care and the importance of maintaining a balanced and healthy lifestyle. Integrating hemp into this routine can enhance its effectiveness and bring a new level of order and purity to their health regimen.

- **Morning Rituals**: Starting the day with a CBD-infused tea or smoothie can set a tone of calm and focus for Virgo. The ritual of preparing these beverages can also satisfy their need for a meticulous start to the morning, aligning with their preference for natural and wholesome ingredients.
- **Fitness and Recovery**: Virgo's dedication to fitness and physical health can be supported by incorporating hemp-based products

into their workout and recovery routines. CBD topicals applied post-exercise can help with muscle soreness and inflammation, complementing Virgo's disciplined approach to physical wellness.

- **Mindful Meditation**: For the detail-oriented Virgo, meditation can sometimes be a challenge due to their active minds. CBD oil or tinctures taken before meditation can aid in calming the mind, making it easier for Virgo to enter a state of deep relaxation and mindfulness, enhancing the quality of their meditative practices.

- **Clean Eating and Cooking**: Virgo's interest in health and cleanliness extends to their diet, making hemp seeds a perfect addition to their culinary repertoire. Rich in protein, omega-3, and fiber, hemp seeds can be sprinkled on salads, blended into dressings, or added to baking, providing nutritional benefits that align with Virgo's health-conscious eating habits.

- **Skincare Routine**: Virgo's attention to detail is apparent in their skincare routine, which can be enhanced with hemp-based products. Hemp oil, known for its anti-inflammatory and moisturizing properties, can be a key component in Virgo's skincare, supporting their pursuit of purity and natural beauty.

Organizing the Herbal Cabinet

True to their nature, Virgos appreciate order and cleanliness in every aspect of their lives, including their use of hemp. Organizing their hemp products, categorizing them by type and use, and maintaining a clean and dedicated space for their herbal supplements can satisfy Virgo's need for structure and cleanliness. This meticulous approach ensures that their wellness routine is not only effective but also harmonious with their overall lifestyle.

Conclusion: Virgo's Path to Purity and Wellness

For Virgo, the Healer's Herb, hemp becomes an integral part of their journey toward health, purity, and balance. By selecting strains and products that align with their health-conscious values and integrating hemp into their meticulous wellness routines, Virgo can enhance their physical and mental well-being. In the Cannabis Galaxy, Virgo's journey is a testament to the healing power of hemp, a reflection of their dedication to wellness, and a celebration of their enduring pursuit of purity and order. With hemp as their ally, Virgo continues to walk a path of health and harmony, guided by the stars and their unwavering commitment to self-care.

If you want to see some amazing products, please visit my Virtual Dispensary: https://shift.store/sg1fan23477/retail

Chapter 8: Libra - The Harmonizer's Blend

As our voyage through the Cannabis Galaxy glides into the realm of Libra, we encounter the essence of balance, harmony, and beauty. Governed by Venus, the planet of love, art, and aesthetics, Libra seeks equilibrium in all things and possesses an innate ability to foster connections and mediate with grace. This chapter reflects on Libra's quest for balance and beauty, exploring how it is mirrored in the harmonious effects of certain hemp strains. Additionally, we offer suggestions for strain pairing and social activities that enhance Libra's natural aptitude for creating equilibrium and nurturing relationships.

Hemp Strains that Echo Libra's Aesthetic

For Libra, the choice of hemp strains is influenced by their pursuit of balance between stimulation and relaxation, aiming for a harmonious state that complements their sociable and artistic nature. Strains such as Wedding Cake and Gelato stand out for their ability to provide a balanced high, soothing the body while invigorating the mind with creative euphoria. These strains embody the essence of Libra's quest for symmetry and beauty, offering a perfect blend of effects that stimulate social interaction and artistic expression.

Strain Pairing for Social Harmony

Libra, the zodiac's social butterfly, thrives in gatherings and events that bring people together. Strain pairing, the art of selecting complementary hemp strains for different moments of a social gathering, can enhance the ambiance and interaction, aligning perfectly with Libra's talent for creating harmonious social settings.

- **Welcome Strains**: As guests arrive, offering a light, uplifting strain like Strawberry Cough can set a joyful and welcoming tone, easing conversations and fostering connections from the start.
- **Dinner Pairings**: For a sit-down dinner, pairing strains with food can elevate the culinary experience. A strain with earthy and piney

notes, such as Pineapple Express, can complement a hearty meal, enhancing flavors and stimulating the palate.

- **After-Dinner Relaxation**: To wind down, a relaxing strain like Lavender, known for its calming effects and sweet floral aroma, can create a tranquil atmosphere, allowing guests to unwind and reflect on the evening's joys.

Libra's Artistic Salons

Inspired by the artistic salons of the past, where intellectuals, artists, and poets gathered to discuss ideas and art, Libra can organize hemp-infused salons. These gatherings can be centered around themes such as poetry readings, art critiques, or musical performances, with selected strains that inspire creativity and deepen appreciation for the arts. This not only caters to Libra's love for aesthetics but also strengthens their role as a connector of like-minded individuals.

Balance in Nature: Outdoor Gatherings

Libra's appreciation for beauty extends to the natural world, making outdoor social activities a delightful setting for fostering connections and enjoying hemp. Organizing picnics in scenic locations or gentle hikes through nature reserves, with hemp strains that enhance the sensory appreciation of the outdoors, can be a rejuvenating experience. Such gatherings celebrate Libra's ability to find balance and harmony in the company of others, amidst the beauty of nature.

Meditative Sessions for Inner Balance

While Libra excels in creating external harmony, they also seek inner balance. Hosting meditative sessions or yoga classes where participants can partake in mild, calming strains beforehand can facilitate a deeper connection with oneself and the universe. This practice aligns with Libra's quest for equilibrium, providing a space for reflection, relaxation, and spiritual alignment.

Conclusion: Libra's Symphony of Harmony

For Libra, the Harmonizer's Blend, hemp becomes an instrument in their symphony of balance, beauty, and connection. Through thoughtful strain selection and pairing, alongside the organization of social activities that foster harmony and artistic expression, Libra can enhance their natural ability to mediate and connect. In the Cannabis Galaxy, Libra's journey is a dance of equilibrium, an artful blend of social grace and aesthetic appreciation, powered by the harmonious effects of hemp. With every step, Libra weaves a tapestry of relationships and beauty, underpinned by their unending pursuit of balance and symmetry.

If you want to see some amazing products, please visit my Virtual Dispensary: https://shift.store/sg1fan23477/retail

Chapter 9: Scorpio - The Mystic's Shadow

Venturing deeper into the enigmatic waters of the Cannabis Galaxy, we find ourselves enveloped in the domain of Scorpio, the zodiac's mystic and shaman. Scorpio is a sign marked by intensity, depth, and a relentless pursuit of truth that lies beneath the surface. Governed by Pluto, the planet of transformation and rebirth, Scorpios are natural investigators of the soul's darker corners and the mysteries that bind the universe. This chapter explores how the transformative Scorpio can utilize potent hemp strains to unlock the mysteries of the self and the universe. Additionally, we will delve into tips for introspective and transformative rituals with cannabis that allow Scorpio to navigate their profound inner waters and embrace their transformative power.

Hemp Strains for the Scorpio Odyssey

For Scorpio, the journey into the self is no light affair—it demands depth, intensity, and the willingness to confront the shadow. Hemp strains that offer potent, introspective highs, such as OG Kush and Gorilla Glue, can serve as key allies in this quest. These strains, known for their deep calming effects and ability to induce profound states of introspection, mirror Scorpio's need for profound emotional and psychological exploration, helping to peel back the layers of the self and the universe.

Rituals of Transformation

Scorpio's path is one of constant transformation, shedding old skins to reveal new truths and strengths. Incorporating cannabis into rituals of transformation can intensify this journey, providing a conduit for deep self-exploration and renewal.

- **Shadow Work Sessions:** Scorpio can harness the introspective power of cannabis in shadow work, a practice aimed at uncovering and integrating the hidden parts of oneself. By setting an intention before partaking in a chosen strain, Scorpio can delve into meditation or journaling, confronting personal fears, desires, and the unconscious mind in a safe, sacred space.

- **Moonlit Rituals**: Aligning cannabis rituals with the phases of the moon can amplify Scorpio's transformative energy, especially during the new and full moons—times of beginning and culmination. In the privacy of the night, under the moon's glow, Scorpio can use these moments to set intentions for personal growth or release what no longer serves their higher purpose, supported by the reflective qualities of their chosen cannabis strain.

- **Water Meditations**: Given Scorpio's affinity for water, meditative baths or showers while under the influence of introspective strains can facilitate emotional cleansing and renewal. The combination of water and cannabis can be a powerful medium for purification, allowing Scorpio to wash away the old and emerge reborn, rejuvenated by their inner journey.

- **Tarot and Divination**: For Scorpio, the mystic of the zodiac, engaging in tarot readings or other forms of divination while under the influence can open doors to deeper understanding and guidance. These practices, enhanced by cannabis, can provide insightful reflections on Scorpio's path, shedding light on their deepest questions and aiding in their transformative journey.

Cannabis-Infused Ancestral Connections

Scorpio's exploration of depth and transformation often leads them to connect with ancestral wisdom and the lineage of the past. Incorporating cannabis into rituals that honor and seek guidance from ancestors can deepen Scorpio's connection to their roots and the collective unconscious, providing strength and wisdom as they navigate their personal transformations.

Conclusion: Scorpio's Journey Through the Shadows

For Scorpio, The Mystic's Shadow, cannabis is more than a plant—it is a tool for exploration, a key to unlocking the deeper mysteries of existence. Through the careful selection of potent strains and the integration of introspective and transformative rituals, Scorpio can navigate the depths of their inner waters, embracing the continual process of death and rebirth that defines their essence. In the Cannabis Galaxy, Scorpio's journey is a testament to the power of self-discovery, the courage to face the shadows, and the transformative potential that lies within the darkness. With cannabis as their guide, Scorpio can traverse the unseen realms, emerging with profound insights and the strength to manifest their most authentic self.

If you want to see some amazing products, please visit my Virtual Dispensary: https://shift.store/sg1fan23477/retail

Chapter 10: Sagittarius - The Explorer's Quest

As we navigate further into the vast expanse of the Cannabis Galaxy, our path is illuminated by the fiery spirit of Sagittarius, the Archer. Governed by Jupiter, the planet of expansion, adventure, and higher learning, Sagittarius embodies the eternal quest for knowledge, freedom, and the exploration of the farthest reaches of both the physical and intellectual worlds. This chapter explores how Sagittarius's adventurous spirit is fueled by hemp strains that inspire growth, freedom, and philosophical exploration. We will also venture into ideas for travel and adventure, both physical and intellectual, that Sagittarians can undertake under the guidance of cannabis, embracing the essence of their boundless curiosity and zest for life.

Hemp Strains for the Sagittarian Spirit

Sagittarius seeks strains that can match their expansive nature, enhancing their quest for wisdom and the joy of discovery. Strains like Durban Poison, with its energizing and uplifting effects, and Amnesia Haze, known for its ability to enhance creativity and stimulate intellectual exploration, are ideal companions for the Sagittarian explorer. These strains not only fuel their adventurous spirit but also open their minds to new perspectives and possibilities, aligning with their love for growth and exploration.

Adventures in the Physical Realm

Sagittarians are natural explorers, not just of the mind but of the world. Cannabis can enhance their physical journeys, adding depth and introspection to their adventures.

- **Cannabis-Infused Nature Treks:** Planning hikes or camping trips in nature reserves or national parks, where the beauty of the earth can be fully appreciated, can be a profound experience for Sagittarius. Selecting strains that heighten sensory perception can make the colors brighter, the landscapes more awe-inspiring, and the connection to the earth deeper.

- **World Exploration with a Twist**: Sagittarius has a penchant for travel and experiencing different cultures. Incorporating cannabis into these travels, where safe and legal, can add an enriching layer to their cultural explorations. Visiting cannabis-friendly destinations and engaging in local traditions and practices can offer new insights and experiences, fueling Sagittarius's love for adventure.

Intellectual Journeys Guided by Cannabis

The quest for knowledge is ever-present in Sagittarius's life. Cannabis can be a catalyst for intellectual expansion and philosophical exploration, opening doors to new realms of thought.

- **Philosophical Discussions and Debates**: Hosting or participating in cannabis-infused philosophical discussions or debates can stimulate Sagittarius's intellect and quench their thirst for wisdom. Engaging with others in conversations about the mysteries of the universe, ethics, and the human experience, enhanced by thought-provoking strains, can lead to profound insights and growth.
- **Cannabis-Enhanced Learning Experiences**: Whether it's attending lectures, workshops, or online courses, Sagittarius can enhance their learning experience with cannabis. Strains that boost focus and creativity can make these educational ventures more engaging and enjoyable, helping Sagittarius to absorb and contemplate new knowledge.

Spiritual Exploration

Sagittarius also embarks on a quest for spiritual growth and understanding. Cannabis can serve as a tool for deepening their spiritual practice, whether through meditation, yoga, or other exploratory practices.

- **Meditative Retreats**: Attending or organizing meditative retreats, where Sagittarians can explore their inner selves and the universe's mysteries, can be significantly enhanced with the use of cannabis. Strains that promote introspection and calm can facilitate deeper meditation, helping Sagittarius connect with their spiritual essence.

- **Yoga and Body Movement**: Integrating cannabis into yoga or other body movement practices can help Sagittarius achieve a greater sense of freedom and body-mind connection, enhancing their physical and spiritual exploration.

Conclusion: The Boundless Journey of Sagittarius

For Sagittarius, The Explorer's Quest is an unending journey of discovery, growth, and freedom. Through the strategic use of cannabis, Sagittarians can enhance their adventures across the physical, intellectual, and spiritual landscapes, finding new horizons within and without. In the Cannabis Galaxy, Sagittarius's path is lit with the flame of curiosity, leading them to explore the deepest mysteries of existence and the farthest reaches of the world. With hemp as their travel companion, Sagittarius continues to soar, embodying the true spirit of exploration and the joy of the quest.

If you want to see some amazing products, please visit my Virtual Dispensary: https://shift.store/sg1fan23477/retail

Chapter 11: Capricorn - The Architect's Foundation

Ascending further into the celestial narrative of the Cannabis Galaxy, we align with the constellation of Capricorn, the zodiac's architect. Ruled by Saturn, the planet of discipline, structure, and long-term achievements, Capricorn embodies the essence of ambition, persistence, and the unwavering drive to build lasting legacies. This chapter outlines how Capricorn's disciplined and ambitious journey is supported by hemp strains that enhance focus and resilience. We also explore structured cannabis meditation and goal-setting practices that empower Capricorn to meticulously construct their dreams, laying a strong foundation for their aspirations to manifest.

Hemp Strains for Capricorn's Steadfast Climb

The journey of Capricorn is marked by steady ascent, requiring focus, determination, and mental clarity. Hemp strains such as Harle-Tsu, with its high CBD content and minimal psychoactive effects, and Cannatonic, known for its focus-enhancing properties, are ideal for Capricorns. These strains provide the mental clarity and resilience needed to navigate challenges without distracting from their goals, supporting Capricorn's natural propensity for hard work and perseverance.

Cannabis-Infused Meditation for Foundation Building

For Capricorn, meditation is not merely a practice for relaxation but a tool for visualization and manifestation. Incorporating cannabis into meditation sessions can deepen the focus and enhance the clarity of their vision, aiding in the construction of their goals.

- **Structured Visualization Sessions**: By engaging in structured visualization sessions enhanced by cannabis, Capricorns can vividly imagine the blueprint of their aspirations. This practice involves meditating on the specific steps needed to achieve their goals, from the foundation up, making the abstract tangible and the intangible concrete.
- **Grounding Rituals**: Cannabis can also aid in grounding rituals

that help Capricorns stay connected to their roots and the practical aspects of their ambitions. Using strains that enhance body awareness, Capricorns can perform grounding exercises that reinforce their connection to the earth, symbolizing the solid foundation upon which they build their dreams.

Goal-Setting Practices with a Cannabis Twist

Capricorn's approach to goal-setting is methodical and precise, mirroring their overall strategy for life. Cannabis can add a creative twist to this process, encouraging innovative solutions to obstacles and enhancing strategic thinking.

- **Cannabis-Enhanced Journaling**: Regular journaling sessions, where Capricorns outline their goals, progress, and reflections, can be augmented with cannabis to stimulate creativity and introspection. This practice can help Capricorns break free from conventional thinking, discovering new paths to their objectives.
- **Strategic Brainstorming Sessions**: Engaging in brainstorming sessions while under the influence of thought-provoking strains can help Capricorns plot the course to their goals. These sessions can be used to identify potential challenges and devise comprehensive strategies to overcome them, ensuring that every base is covered.

Building Community and Networks

Understanding the importance of support systems in achieving greatness, Capricorns can use cannabis as a tool to strengthen bonds within their professional and personal networks.

- **Cannabis Networking Events**: Organizing or participating in cannabis-infused networking events can provide Capricorns with the opportunity to connect with like-minded individuals. These gatherings can serve as a platform for sharing ideas, resources, and support, reinforcing the collective foundation upon which individual success is built.

- **Team Building and Collaboration**: For projects requiring teamwork, cannabis can facilitate a harmonious collaboration environment. Sessions designed to enhance group cohesion and brainstorming can benefit from strains that promote empathy and open communication, aligning team members with the project's vision and goals.

Conclusion: Capricorn's Ascent on the Architect's Foundation

For Capricorn, the Architect's Foundation, cannabis serves as both a tool for enhanced focus and a medium for creative strategy in the construction of their ambitions. By choosing strains that support mental clarity and resilience, and incorporating cannabis into meditation and goal-setting practices, Capricorn can fortify the foundation upon which their dreams are built. In the Cannabis Galaxy, Capricorn's journey is a testament to the power of discipline, structure, and the undying spirit of ambition. With hemp as their ally, Capricorns are equipped to ascend to the greatest heights, building their legacy one stone at a time, anchored in the solid ground of their unwavering resolve and visionary planning.

If you want to see some amazing products, please visit my Virtual Dispensary: https://shift.store/sg1fan23477/retail

Chapter 12: Aquarius - The Visionary's Vision

Our celestial journey through the Cannabis Galaxy culminates in the sign of Aquarius, where the waters of innovation and humanity flow freely. Ruled by Uranus, the planet of breakthroughs and future visions, Aquarius embodies the spirit of innovation, community, and the relentless pursuit of social progress. This chapter delves into how Aquarius's innovative and humanitarian nature is elevated by hemp strains that foster creativity and collective well-being. We will also explore community-focused cannabis activities and brainstorming sessions that empower Aquarius to lead the charge in pioneering social change, staying true to their role as the zodiac's visionary.

Hemp Strains for the Aquarian Mind

The Aquarian mind thrives on creativity, originality, and the exploration of new horizons. Hemp strains such as Super Silver Haze, known for its invigorating cerebral effects, and Blue Dream, celebrated for its balance of euphoria and full-body relaxation, are particularly suited to Aquarians. These strains stimulate the creative process, open the mind to unconventional ideas, and enhance the visionary's capacity for innovation, perfectly aligning with Aquarius's futuristic outlook.

Innovative Community Engagement

Aquarius is deeply connected to the collective, always seeking ways to contribute to societal advancement and the common good. Integrating cannabis into community-focused activities can amplify their impact, bringing together like-minded individuals to collaborate on projects that reflect their shared ideals.

- **Cannabis and Creativity Workshops**: Organizing workshops that combine cannabis with creative expression can serve as powerful incubators for innovative ideas. Whether it's art, music, writing, or another form of creative output, these gatherings can stimulate new ways of thinking and problem-solving, encouraging participants to envision and create a better future.

- **Sustainability and Hemp**: Aquarius's concern for the future of the planet makes them passionate about sustainability. Initiatives that explore the use of hemp in sustainable practices, such as biodegradable plastics, eco-friendly clothing, and renewable resources, can be a fertile ground for Aquarian innovation. Hosting seminars or workshops that focus on hemp's role in sustainability can inspire practical solutions to environmental challenges.

Brainstorming Sessions for Social Change

Aquarius excels in conceptualizing ideas that challenge the status quo and pave the way for progress. Cannabis-enhanced brainstorming sessions focused on social change can harness Aquarius's visionary thinking, turning abstract ideas into actionable plans.

- **Think Tanks for Humanity**: Creating think tanks or discussion groups where cannabis is used as a tool to facilitate open-mindedness and out-of-the-box thinking can be incredibly fruitful for Aquarians. These sessions can focus on pressing global issues, exploring innovative solutions to problems like inequality, climate change, and human rights.

- **Cannabis-Infused Social Activism**: Aquarius is naturally drawn to social activism, and incorporating cannabis into activism strategies can open new avenues for awareness and engagement. Whether it's through art installations, public demonstrations, or awareness campaigns, using cannabis as a medium to convey messages can add a unique and impactful dimension to Aquarian efforts for change.

Digital Platforms for Collective Ideation

In today's digital age, Aquarius can leverage technology to widen their reach and amplify their impact. Establishing online platforms where cannabis enthusiasts and visionaries can congregate to share ideas, projects, and innovations can foster a global community of like-minded individuals. Virtual brainstorming sessions, webinars, and collaborative projects facilitated through these platforms can break geographical barriers, uniting people around shared goals and visions for the future.

Conclusion: Aquarius's Role as the Architect of Tomorrow

For Aquarius, The Visionary's Vision, cannabis is not just a plant but a catalyst for innovation, community building, and social progress. By selecting strains that enhance creativity and collective well-being, and engaging in community-focused activities and brainstorming sessions, Aquarius can channel their boundless energy and ideas into tangible change. In the Cannabis Galaxy, Aquarius stands as a beacon of hope and progress, guiding humanity toward a brighter, more inclusive future. With hemp as their companion, Aquarians continue to dream, innovate, and inspire, weaving the fabric of a new world with every thought, every action, and every vision shared.

If you want to see some amazing products, please visit my Virtual Dispensary: https://shift.store/sg1fan23477/retailTop

Chapter 13: Pisces - The Dreamer's Delight

As we draw our astrological adventure through the Cannabis Galaxy to a close, we immerse ourselves in the mystical waters of Pisces. This final constellation in the zodiac is where the boundaries between the physical and spiritual realms dissolve, and the essence of empathy, creativity, and dreamlike introspection comes to the fore. Ruled by Neptune, the planet of dreams, illusions, and higher spiritual connections, Pisces embodies the soul of the artist, the empath, and the eternal dreamer. This chapter delves into how Pisces's deep connection to the spiritual and emotional realms is enhanced by dreamy, introspective hemp strains. Furthermore, we explore artistic and spiritual cannabis practices that allow Pisces to navigate and thrive within their vast seas of imagination and empathy.

Hemp Strains for Pisces's Ethereal Journey

To complement the ethereal and introspective nature of Pisces, certain hemp strains stand out for their ability to deepen the connection to the spiritual and emotional realms. Strains like Granddaddy Purple and Northern Lights offer a soothing, dreamlike state, ideal for Pisces's reflective and introspective moments. These strains facilitate a journey into the subconscious, unlocking dreams and enhancing spiritual insights, aligning perfectly with Pisces's desire for deep emotional and spiritual exploration.

Cannabis-Infused Artistic Expression

Pisces's soul is intrinsically linked to the realms of art and creativity, where they find a powerful outlet for their boundless imagination and empathy. Integrating cannabis into their artistic practices can elevate their natural talents and open new avenues of inspiration.

- **Painting and Drawing Sessions**: Under the influence of inspiring strains, Pisces can engage in painting or drawing sessions that allow them to visually express the depths of their emotions and the visions of their dreams. The enhanced creativity and lowered inhibitions can lead to the creation of profoundly personal and transcendent works of art.
- **Music and Cannabis Harmony**: For Pisces, music is both a refuge and a form of expression. Playing or listening to music while enjoying strains that amplify emotional sensitivity can be a deeply moving and healing experience. This practice can help Pisces connect more deeply with the music, experiencing it as a true expression of the soul.

Spiritual Practices with a Cannabis Twist

Pisces's spiritual journey is a core aspect of their being, seeking connections with the divine and the universal consciousness. Cannabis can serve as a catalyst in these spiritual explorations, enhancing the depth and intensity of their practices.

- **Meditative Journeys**: Incorporating cannabis into meditation can help Pisces achieve deeper states of relaxation and introspection, facilitating encounters with their higher selves and the spiritual realm. This can be especially powerful during practices aimed at visualization, healing, or connecting with the universal energy.
- **Yoga and Mindfulness**: Engaging in yoga or mindfulness practices while under the influence of cannabis strains that promote body awareness can help Pisces feel more connected to the physical and spiritual worlds. This synergy between movement, breath, and heightened sensory perception can deepen their yoga practice, bringing about a greater sense of harmony and inner peace.

Dream Exploration and Journaling

Pisces is naturally attuned to the world of dreams, often receiving insights and inspiration from the subconscious. Cannabis can intensify this connection, making dreams more vivid and easier to recall.

- **Dream Journaling**: Keeping a dream journal beside the bed to record insights and visions from cannabis-enhanced dreams can be a valuable practice for Pisces. This can help them decode messages from the subconscious, offering guidance, creativity, and understanding.
- **Lucid Dreaming Practices**: For those Pisces interested in exploring lucid dreaming, certain cannabis strains can be utilized to increase the likelihood of achieving lucidity. Engaging in pre-sleep meditation or visualization techniques while under the influence can prepare the mind for a conscious exploration of the dream world.

Conclusion: Navigating Pisces's Ocean of Dreams

For Pisces, The Dreamer's Delight, cannabis acts as a vessel, navigating the deep and often turbulent waters of their imagination, emotions, and spirituality. By selecting strains that enhance introspection and creativity, and incorporating cannabis into their artistic and spiritual practices, Pisces can enrich their journey through the realms of dreams and empathy. In the Cannabis Galaxy, Pisces's path is illuminated by the soft glow of the stars, guiding them through their vast internal seascape. With cannabis as their compass, Pisces can explore the depths of their being, uncovering hidden treasures of insight, creativity, and spiritual enlightenment, embracing the infinite possibilities of their ethereal voyage.

If you want to see some amazing products, please visit my Virtual Dispensary: https://shift.store/sg1fan23477/retail

Conclusion: Hemp's Journey Through the Zodiac

As we conclude our celestial odyssey through the Cannabis Galaxy, we find ourselves enriched with a deeper understanding of the intricate tapestry that weaves together the cosmos, the zodiac, and the versatile, magical plant known as hemp. This journey has taken us through the unique landscapes of each zodiac sign, revealing the special connection each has with hemp and how this ancient plant can amplify our strengths, soothe our weaknesses, and enhance our innate characteristics.

From the fiery ambition of Aries to the dreamy depths of Pisces, hemp emerges as a versatile ally, capable of adapting its benefits to match the needs and aspirations of each sign. We have seen how hemp strains can fuel the warrior spirit of Aries, stabilize the steadfast determination of Taurus, invigorate the intellectual curiosity of Gemini, and soothe the emotional tides of Cancer. Leo's radiant warmth was magnified, Virgo's meticulous nature supported, Libra's quest for harmony balanced, and Scorpio's depth of introspection deepened, all through the mindful integration of cannabis. Sagittarius's adventurous journey was expanded, Capricorn's disciplined ascent bolstered, Aquarius's innovative visions uplifted, and Pisces's spiritual voyage deepened, showcasing the plant's remarkable adaptability and its potential to enhance our human experience.

This astrological adventure through the Cannabis Galaxy illuminates the profound synergy between our zodiacal blueprints and cannabis, a relationship that transcends mere recreation to touch upon the spiritual, emotional, and intellectual realms. It encourages us to continue exploring this synergy, fostering a deeper understanding of ourselves, the cosmos, and the magical plant that links them.

As we navigate our personal astrological landscapes, let us remember that the journey with cannabis, like the journey through life, is deeply personal and infinitely varied. The exploration of this connection offers not just a path to personal well-being but also a means of connecting with the universe's larger rhythms and energies. It's an invitation to experiment, to learn, and to grow, always mindful of the intent and respect we bring to these practices.

In embracing the celestial guidance offered by our astrological signs and the enhancing properties of hemp, we unlock new dimensions of our being. We discover tools for healing, creativity, and personal evolution, forging a bond with the natural world that is both ancient and profoundly relevant to our modern lives.

The journey does not end here; it evolves and expands as we do. As the cosmos shifts and turns, so too do our needs, dreams, and the ways in which cannabis can serve as a companion and guide. We are encouraged to keep exploring, keep questioning, and keep aligning with the vibrations of the universe, finding in hemp a sacred ally on our path through the stars.

In this adventure through the Cannabis Galaxy, we've navigated the celestial influences of the zodiac, uncovering the profound connections between the stars, our souls, and cannabis. This exploration is but the beginning of a larger journey, one that invites each of us to delve deeper into our cosmic blueprint, engage with the healing and transformative powers of hemp, and embrace the boundless potential within us. As we continue on our paths, let us carry the wisdom, insights, and inspirations from this journey, using them to light our way as we explore the infinite possibilities that lie at the intersection of astrology, cannabis, and the human spirit.

Further Reading and Resources

Embarking on "Hemp in The Houses: An Astrological Adventure Through the Cannabis Galaxy" has opened up a universe of connections between the cosmos, our inner selves, and the ancient plant of hemp. For those eager to delve deeper into the mysteries and practicalities of astrology, cannabis cultivation, its medicinal uses, and the spiritual dimensions of cannabis use, the journey is just beginning. Below is a curated collection of resources designed to guide you further on this path of discovery.

Recommended Readings

1. **Astrology and Personal Growth**
   - "The Only Astrology Book You'll Ever Need" by Joanna Martine Woolfolk: An essential guide for anyone looking to understand the basics of astrology and how it applies to their personal life, relationships, and growth.
   - "Astrology for the Soul" by Jan Spiller: A profound exploration of the North Node and its astrological significance, offering insights into soul growth and life lessons.

2. **Cannabis Cultivation and Use**
   - "The Cannabis Grow Bible: The Definitive Guide to Growing Marijuana for Recreational and Medicinal Use" by Greg Green: Offers comprehensive knowledge on cultivating cannabis, covering everything from the basics to advanced techniques.
   - "Cannabis Pharmacy: The Practical Guide to Medical Marijuana" by Michael Backes: Provides in-depth information on the medicinal use of cannabis, including the science behind how it works and advice on personalizing usage.

3. **Spiritual and Medicinal Aspects of Cannabis**
   - "The Pot Book: A Complete Guide to Cannabis" edited by Julie Holland, M.D.: Explores the role of cannabis in

medicine, politics, history, and society, with contributions from experts across various fields.

- "Cannabis and Spirituality: An Explorer's Guide to an Ancient Plant Spirit Ally" edited by Stephen Gray: A comprehensive guide to the spiritual benefits and applications of cannabis, including historical perspectives and contemporary testimonials.

Websites

1. **Astrology Insights**
   - Astro.com: Offers free birth charts, personal horoscopes, and extensive articles on astrology, helping individuals understand their astrological profiles.
   - CafeAstrology.com: A resource for those seeking to learn more about astrology, providing detailed interpretations of zodiac signs, planetary movements, and astrological events.

2. **Cannabis Knowledge**
   - Leafly.com: A leading online resource for cannabis information, strain reviews, and dispensary locations, ideal for both medicinal and recreational users.
   - ProjectCBD.org: Focused on the medicinal aspects of cannabis, especially CBD, offering research, guidance, and patient stories.

Forums and Communities

1. **Astrology Forums**
   - Reddit - r/astrology: A community where astrology enthusiasts gather to discuss astrological influences, share personal experiences, and seek advice.
   - AstroSeek.com Forums: Provides a platform for discussions on various astrological topics, from beginner questions to advanced theoretical debates.

2. Cannabis Cultivation and Spirituality

- ◦ Grasscity Forums: Features a section dedicated to the cultivation of cannabis, with threads on grow guides, troubleshooting, and strain recommendations.
- ◦ Reddit - r/cannabis: A community for sharing news, experiences, and discussions on the cultivation, medicinal use, and legalization of cannabis.

By exploring these resources, enthusiasts can deepen their understanding of the intricate dance between the stars and cannabis. Whether your interest lies in the personal insights astrology offers, the art and science of cannabis cultivation, its medicinal properties, or the spiritual awakening it can facilitate, there is a wealth of knowledge waiting to be discovered. "Hemp in The Houses: An Astrological Adventure Through the Cannabis Galaxy" is just the beginning. The journey of exploration, understanding, and personal growth continues as you dive deeper into the realms of astrology and cannabis, uncovering new layers of wisdom and connection in the universe's grand design.

<u>Message from the Author:</u>

I hope you enjoyed this book, I love astrology and knew there was not a book such as this out on the shelf. I love metaphysical items as well. Please check out my other books:

-Life of Government Benefits

-My life of Hell

-My life with Hydrocephalus

-Red Sky

-World Domination:Woman's rule

-World Domination:Woman's Rule 2: The War

-Life and Banishment of Apophis: book 1

-The Kidney Friendly Diet

-The Ultimate Hemp Cookbook

-Creating a Dispensary(legally)

-Cleanliness throughout life: the importance of showering from child-hood to adulthood.

-Strong Roots: The Risks of Overcoddling children

-Hemp Horoscopes: Cosmic Insights and Earthly Healing

- Celestial Hemp Navigating the Zodiac: Through the Green Cosmos

-Astrological Hemp: Aligning The Stars with Earth's Ancient Herb

-The Astrological Guide to Hemp: Stars, Signs, and Sacred Leaves

-Green Growth: Innovative Marketing Strategies for your Hemp Products and Dispensary

-Cosmic Cannabis

-Astrological Munchies

-Henry The Hemp

-Zodiacal Roots: The Astrological Soul Of Hemp

- **Green Constellations: Intersection of Hemp and Zodiac**

Check out my Virtual dispensary for all your hemp needs: https://shift.store/sg1fan23477/retail

If you want solar for your home go here: https://www.harborsolar.live/apophisenterprises/

Instagrams: @apophis_enterprises, @hempkingdom2024, @apophisbookemporium, @apophisfashion, @apophisscardshop

Twitter: @apophisenterpr1, Tiktok:@apophisenterprise

Youtube: @sg1fan23477

Podcast: Apophis Chat Zone: https://open.spotify.com/show/5zXbrCLEV2xzCp8ybrfHsk?si=fb4d4fdbdce44dec

Newsletter: https://apophiss-newsletter-27c897.beehiiv.com/